# SAP Security Interview Questions, Answers, and Explanations

## By SAPCOOKBOOK.COM

SAP Security Interview Questions, Answers, and Explanations

ISBN 10: 1-933804-96-3
ISBN 13: 978-1-933804-96-5

Edited By: Jamie Fisher

Copyright© 2006
Revised 2007

Printed in the United States of America

Please visit our website at www.sapcookbook.com

# Table of Contents

Motivation...................................................................................7

Introduction............................................................................ 8

Question 1: Role Naming Procedures................................... 9

Question 2: Display Only SM59........................................... 11

Question 3: APO Authorizations ......................................... 11

Question 4: Tcode /SAPAPO/SDP94....................................12

Question 5: Comparing user assignments .........................12

Question 6: Table names.......................................................13

Question 7: Cost center field in SU01.................................13

Question 8: Security report scheduling...............................14

Question 9: Querying restricted roles .................................14

Question 10: Accidental deletions .......................................15

Question 11: Accidental deletions 2.....................................15

Question 12: Conflicting combinations ...............................16

Question 13: The Parameters tab ........................................16

Question 14: Org Level Tables .............................................17

Question 15: Setting values in authorization objects..............17

Question 16: Authorization reports .....................................18

Question 17: Movement types..............................................18

Question 18: Login/disable_multi_gui_login......................19

Question 19: Expert mode....................................................19

Question 20: Accessing authorization objects ....................... 20

Question 21: Display transaction code in PFCG? .................. 20

Question 22: Upgrading issues.............................................21

Question 23: ITAR Issues ....................................................21

Question 24: ABAP Authority check ................................... 22

Question 25: Disable billing blocks .................................... 22

Question 26: Disable SPRO ................................................ 23

Question 27: Restricting access from MM03........................ 23

Question 28: Creating new CATT in 6.4 .............................. 24

Question 29: Changing doc types ........................................ 24

Question 30: Transaction code access ................................ 25

Question 31: Authorization object V_VBAK_VKO .............. 25

Question 32: Accidental authorization................................ 26

Question 33: Tracking user data.......................................... 26

Question 34: Changing user defaults ................................... 27

Question 35: Changing authorization group names............. 28

Question 36: Authorizing hierarchies ................................. 28

Question 37: BDC user vs. service user ............................... 29

Question 38: RESPAREA...................................................... 29

Question 39: HR go-live....................................................... 30

Question 40: Field values in auth groups ............................. 31
Question 41: CCMS Configuration ...................................... 32
Question 42: FICO SME ..................................................... 33
Question 43: Self-service password reset ........................... 34
Question 44: Transaction VF02 ......................................... 34
Question 45: Remote copy ................................................. 35
Question 46: Surveying departments ................................. 35
Question 47: Op SAP PS .................................................... 36
Question 48: Transaction execution .................................. 37
Question 49: Auth object f_lfa1_grp ................................. 37
Question 50: Query group in QuickViewer ......................... 38
Question 51: Critical combinations ................................... 39
Question 52: Creating a role in SAP CRM ......................... 40
Question 53: Specialized login problems .......................... 41
Question 54: Executing ST03 ............................................ 42
Question 55: Turning off modify data ............................... 42
Question 56: Cross module roles ...................................... 43
Question 57: Role FBL3N .................................................. 44
Question 58: Object F_IT_ALV .......................................... 45
Question 59: Transaction PV7I .......................................... 46
Question 60: Building roles in PFCG .................................. 47
Question 61: Management roles ........................................ 47
Question 62: User comparison .......................................... 48
Question 63: List personnel areas ..................................... 48
Question 64: Transaction codes FS00/FSP0 ...................... 49
Question 65: Assigned role in child system ....................... 50
Question 66: Db-tab TCURR .............................................. 50
Question 67: Executable transactions ............................... 51
Question 68: PHAP_SEARCH_PA ...................................... 51
Question 69: Restrict Report Variant access ..................... 52
Question 70: Overwrite user authorizations ..................... 52
Question 71: Restrict ME21 ............................................... 53
Question 72: Content repository ....................................... 54
Question 73: Download list of all SAP transactions .......... 54
Question 74: Finding tables .............................................. 55
Question 75: User authorizations ...................................... 56
Question 76: Security - Material Master ............................. 57
Question 77: Super-user authority for emergencies .......... 58
Question 78: CUA for R/3, BW. APO .................................. 60
Question 79: Authorization of VA02 .................................. 61
Question 80: Authorization ............................................... 62
Question 81: Restricting access to certain fields .............. 64
Question 82: AR - Creating customer master data ............ 65

Question 83: Possible values for customer authn grp.......... 66
Question 84: Authorizations for settings ............... 67
Question 85: CATT ................ 67
Question 86: A list of all PM transactions - 46C ............... 68
Question 87: Authorizations - Transaction CAT2 ............... 69
Question 88: Profiles deleted ............... 70
Question 89: Transaction Report - Roles............... 71
Question 90: Tracing security authorizations in BEX Analyzer73
Question 91: Authorization object for a t-code ............... 73
Question 92: Restriction on personnel number within CAT274
Question 93: SM35 guidelines ............... 74
Question 94: Profiles for super user............... 75
Question 95: KE5Z Code restrictions on PC line items......... 76
Question 96: Retrieve autho profiles - specific co. code ........ 77
Question 97: Restricting access by organizational unit ........ 78
Question 98: Auth in Transaction sm12 ............... 79
Question 99: General concept - CUA + security best practice80
Question 100: Transfer authorizations and roles of a user... 82
Question 101: When to reset the User Buffer............... 82
Question 102: Background jobs (SA38) ............... 83
Question 103: Keep or transport Favorites on another system84
Question 104: user master compare............... 87
Question 105: Display Authorization for Customization ...... 88
Question 106: Profile Deletion - Role Mass Comparison...... 89
Question 107: Urgent - Authorization ............... 91
Question 108: Authorization for field BLART ............... 92
Question 109: Standard Menu and User Menu Options ....... 93
Question 110: Updating Org Levels in Profile Generator...... 94
Question 111: Authorization in transaction SA38............... 95
Question 112: authorization for testing ............... 97
Question 113: SAP_ALL Dilemma............... 98
Question 114: Authorization for entry only thru program .... 99
Question 115: Mass Deletion of Roles ............... 101
Question 116: Role in CUA and DEV Client ............... 102
Question 117: CAT2 (Timesheet) again: object P_PERNR . 103
Question 118: T-code specified display ............... 104
Question 119: FB02 - Document change............... 105
Question 120: Generate activity group in Production client106
Question 121: PFUD ............... 107
Question 122: MEDRUCK............... 109
Question 123: MK01 Create Vendor ............... 111
Question 124: BEx No Authorization Problem............... 112
Question 125: PAYROLL SECURITY ............... 113

Index ........................................................................ 114

# Motivation

I have found that a lot of the materials available in SAP security are 1) nonexistent 2) too general and pedantic in nature 3) sales materials in disguise. And since there are a very limited number of published books in the area of SAP security, this title was a natural addition to our growing library of practical references for SAP consultants and managers.

This book, SAP Security Essentials, started as a list of particularly useful FAQs in the area of SAP security. That is to say, this is a list of tips and tricks that I have used on projects in the past and thought were good enough to include in a book. So for this book, we are calling each tip, trick, recipe, an "essential."

I hope these SAP Security Essentials are as valuable to you as they have been to me.

# Introduction

Each Question has a question (problem), and an answer – that is pretty straightforward – but when you see the guru icon, this is information that represents the highest degree of knowledge and understanding in a particular area. So be aware that to completely understand any given issue, you should read beyond the first answer.

The Security Guru has Spoken!

# Question 1: Role Naming Procedures

I am trying to determine the best role naming procedures. We are doing a security set-up redesign and would like to use "Generally Accepted Security Role Naming Practices." We are a global company with decentralized SAP set-up with SAP instances for each region.

**A:** The intent of developing a naming convention for SAP access is to facilitate long-term maintenance of Security, enhance auditing features, and improve the periodic review of access. The following is a proposal for the naming convention guidelines for Roles, Profiles and Authorizations. Note: Composite Role naming conventions are not covered as they are NOT recommended for use.

Naming Conventions: Roles 'Z' or 'Y' is not needed as part of the naming convention. SAP Security is Master Data, not configuration or repository object and therefore does not need the standard development name space. The ':' is the customer designation.

Role name template: xxxx;yyyy_Describe_org.
Designate xxxx as major company division, (i.e, Jones, Inc., Parts, etc.). : is the Customer Role designation;
yyyy is the Functional area in SAP such as Financial Accounts Payable (FIAP) or Materials Management Warehouse Maintenance (MMWM).

Under Describe give brief description of Role, i.e., INVOICE_PROCESSOR; Org is any major organizational designations such as plant, sales org or warehouse.

Example: J:FIAP_INVOICE_PROCESSOR is Jones, Inc. Financial Accounts Payable Invoice Processor for the company.

Jones, Inc. is the company, so there is no need to use the _org designation. If this role did ALL or cross company, then a designation would be needed.

Note: If you set the configuration for Session Manager to sort the roles for display, they sort in alphabetical order by technical name. Your generic System roles (Printing, RFC, GUI control, SU56, SU53, SU3, SMX) should sort to the bottom; yyyy should be Cross Application, or XA.

# Question 2: Display Only SM59

SM59 text mentions it can be used for Display/Maintain RFC Connections, how can you make this transaction code display only?

**A:** SM59 is for Display AND Change. There is no display only version. Sorry, it can't be done.

# Question 3: APO Authorizations

Regarding APO authorizations, can you limit to display only in the product master using transaction code /SAPAPO/MAT1?

**A:** For the /SAPAPO/MAT1, make sure you have only 03 on C_APO_PROD.

# Question 4: Tcode /SAPAPO/SDP94

In the planning book screen, certain buttons are missing when using tcode /SAPAPO/SDP94. Neither the "Selection Window" nor the "Display Dependant Objects" buttons are visible.

**A:** Maintain C_APO_FUN to have C_SELCTION, C_SELE and C_SELORG on field APO_FUNC and the name of the planning area on APO_PAREA to make sure /SAPAPO/SDP94 is fully functional and viewable.

# Question 5: Comparing user assignments

How do you compare two user's role assignments? (i.e., What roles is user FOO missing to have exactly the same roles as user BAR?)

**A:** In tcode SUIM there is a report to compare users/ roles and selected output.

The best way to make user BAR have the same access as user FOO is to have one role with the access and assign it to each of them once in tcode SU01. Ensure that this is the only role they have.
If this becomes too complicated, use a program to read in the AGR_USERS tables for two users, and lay out the role assignments side by side showing where the role assignment gaps are.

# Question 6: Table names

What is the table name which houses the full list of activities? (01 change, 02, 03 display, etc...)?

**A:** The table is TACT. Possible activities for one authorized object is: TACTZ.

The list of additional activities is extensive. Go to the profile generator/authorizations screen, pick up any autho object and get to the selection screen for possible activities. Right click and you will see "More values - F7" for a complete list of activities.

Note: May not work for all "activity" fields. In the field for F_REGU_BUK, for example, the values are kept are in a pull-down menu in the transaction F110.

# Question 7: Cost center field in SU01

What is the purpose of the cost center field in the SU01 user master record?

**A:** It is most likely used to allocate costs of system usage to cost centers. Some use it for internal reporting. It is accessible in some of the ALV reports in SUIM.

# Question 8: Security report scheduling

Are there any periodic security reports that need to be scheduled to monitor during maintenance?

**A:** Try running user compare - RHAUTUPD_NEW
SUIM table sync - SUSR_SYNC_USER_TABLES

Other valuable reports:

USTxx Sync to USRxxx (custom program)
RHPROFL0 (for security by position)
Lock/delete inactive users (custom program)
Delete orphaned authorizations/profile (custom program)
Delete orphaned address info.
RHAUTUPD_NEW
Critical User monitoring report and notification (custom program)

# Question 9: Querying restricted roles

Is it possible to query all roles that have a particular Organizational Level Restriction? (e.g. Company Code, Plant, Division, etc.?)

**A:** You can get all the roles that have an authorization for a particular object that contain a company code or plant or other authorization value. Those reports are in transaction SUIM.

# Question 10: Accidental deletions

Users in our system were deleted when they shouldn't have been. To determine how this happened, can I retrace the function or is it logged on a table?

**A:** Debug or use RSUSR100 to find the information.

# Question 11: Accidental deletions 2

While working in development server, my session was deleted by another user. Is there a way to find the user that deleted it, the system number and the related data?

**A:** Try using TX STAT (or STAD, depends on release) and look for someone who has used TX SM04.
With that, you can kill the session. If more than one user has used the same tcode at the given time, SM21 has the entry logged for it.

You can find who ran SM04 and delete that user's session.

# Question 12: Conflicting combinations

How do you find the typical conflicting combinations of authorization objects in HR, like conflicting tcodes, infotypes and clusters?

**A:** If you are looking for conflicts within HR, there aren't many. Some companies use security measures to limit payroll information, update disciplinary actions, promotion potential and medical to specific individuals. It is not done with tcodes, but with limited Info types.
SAP HR is written as a central set of tcodes with access limited by data.
The main tcodes are PA40, PA30 and PA20, HR org management is the PA10, PA03, PA13 or the POME and "run Payroll".

Concentrate on the Info types not necessarily the tcodes not objects as they all use P_ORGIN (or what you configure). The only anomaly is P_ABAP which can override P_ORGIN.

# Question 13: The Parameters tab

What is the "Parameters" tab in the SU01 user maintenance screen for?

**A:** The "Parameters" tab allows users to pre-set entries in order to fill field values in tcodes without having to re-key. Also used for "Set Preferences."

# Question 14: Org Level Tables

Is there a comprehensive list of all the Org Level Tables?

**A:** Try table AUTHX via SE16.

If it is not loaded or incomplete, use the underlying source structures in SE11, including structures: AUTHA, AUTHB, AUTHC and a few others (search on AUTH*). Look for the Check table or value tables. Note: If AUTHX is not loaded, there is a report to load it.

# Question 15: Setting values in authorization objects

When setting values in an auth obj, is there a way to exclude a specific value without compromising the access of the others? Example: I'm trying to restrict S_TABU_DIS to allow certain people to see all the auth groups except SS. If someone creates an auth group in the system, we want the people with this role to see the added group without us going back into the role and adding the value via pfcg.

**A:** Set the values to be included - 00 to SR and ST to ZZ, this would exclude SS.

# Question 16: Authorization reports

How are authorization reports generated? The reports should include activity by object and be accessible to all users with access.

**A:** Run SUSR_SYNC_USER_TABLES and then try tcode SUIM/report RSUSR002. Enter your object in Object 1 and press enter. Follow the prompts.

# Question 17: Movement types

How do you restrict users on Movement types and certain storage locations in transaction MB1B? The only object displayed in SU24 for MB1B, with a combination of Movement type and Storage location, is M_MSEG_LGO. How do we enable the system to check this object in MB1B? Or, how can we restrict users on a combination of Storage location and Movement type in transaction MB1B?

**A:** Storage location must be configured to check authorization on each storage location. SAP does not do this by default so there is no ST01 trace of it until you configure it. This is done in the IMG (tcode SPRO).

If you get the help documentation of M_MSEG_LGO (using SU21), there is a link with the correct customizing tcode which turn on/off the authority check on it (under material management-stocks)

This works only for good movements, not for display stocks content.

# Question 18:
# Login/disable_multi_gui_login

Will activating parameter login/disable_multi_gui_login affect workflow?

**A:** No, the key is the GUI in the parameter. Workflow does not initiate a GUI logon but a logon in the "background" or via RFC to a non-GUI display session.

 **Note:** This parameter is for multiple GUI logins via the SAP Logon Pad or equivalent.

# Question 19: Expert mode

What is the Expert mode in Profile generation? What are the options for its use?

**A:** Expert mode merges existing authorizations with new auths as they are added to the role. The auths display tells you which authorization objects have been added or changed. This is a time-saver in that it clearly lists changes and what to maintain.

 **Note:** Always work in Expert mode.

# Question 20: Accessing authorization objects

Is there a table where I can access the name of a particular Authorization Object? Possibly a SUIM report?

**A:** Start with SU24; it will give the objects/transactions in pfcg use.

After SU24 there are tables USOBT_C and USOBX_C.
SU25, Step 1 is mandatory to initialize these tables. Note: Read Help carefully before executing SU25, Step 1.

# Question 21: Display transaction code in PFCG?

How do you display the transaction code in the Menu folder using PFCG?

**A:** With and existing role, the transactions may be entered straight into the S_TCODE auth object, not the menu.
If the subfolder "Menu" in PFCG displays the list of transactions with only text appearing and not transaction codes, the option needs to be changed.
Go to the right of the screen, beneath the menu tabs and next to the print icon, you will see an icon in the shape of a magnifying glass with either a - or a + symbol in it. Click on that to turn technical names on and off

# Question 22: Upgrading issues

What steps to I take to avoid any security issues that might result when upgrading from SAP 4.6c?

**A:** Run SU25 Steps 2a...2c.

# Question 23: ITAR Issues

Does SAP Security have specific recommendations for maintaining International Traffic in Arms Regulations (ITAR)?

**A:** Your ITAR restrictions are specific to your company. However, the existing SAP methods of restrictions should work as well, except in the PS module in 4.6C. In that case, some custom modifications to restrict Projects and WBS elements may be needed.

Note: Be sure to keep detailed documentation of your role design, testing and monitor/review plans in the event of a government (DCAA & DCMA) audit.

# Question 24: ABAP Authority check

How is the ABAP AUTHORITY-CHECK statement used?

**A:** It checks and divulges authority information in SAP reports. You can also access through a search engine by typing "authority-check" ABAP (or similar).

Go to an ABAP program; click once on AUTHORITY-CHECK. Press F1.

# Question 25: Disable billing blocks

How can we disable the Billing Block field on the Sales tab in the Sales Order in VA02, SAP 4.6c?

**A:** Use V_VBAK_AAT/02.

# Question 26: Disable SPRO

Is it possible to disable customizing (SPRO) for a certain client while enabling changes in tcode OB52 at the same time?

**A:** To disable SPRO: Set your client to "Production" and reset changes to "No Changes Allowed." OB52 will be maintainable, with the exception of the tcodes that automatically change when Production is set.

**Note:** There may be some variance in older versions; in that case, use SOBJ to update your OB52 setting.

# Question 27: Restricting access from MM03

How can we restrict access to the "Current" and "Previous" buttons from the MM03 Costing 2 tab?

**A:** Set authorization groups on BOM; this should block those without display access. The authorization group field must be populated for the BOM

# Question 28: Creating new CATT in 6.4

Can you create a new catt in 6.4? I get a message to use ecatt instead. I created the test script but cannot figure out the variant. My thought is to create a variant for export. I could populate the fields in the text file and run the test config that runs that script and updates user i.d.'s.

**A:** You need to define recording parameters. Create a data container with the same parameters and input your values. To execute, use the test configuration to combine the test script and data container together.

# Question 29: Changing doc types

A user needs to change a doc type 001 for auth group 1; another needs to display doc type 002 for auth group 2. Currently, they can change and display both.

**A:** If there is an auth group for each doc type and you want to change and display in one role, you need to copy the object in the role (Edit->copy authorizations). In one object put change activity for auth group 1, in the other object put display for auth group 2.
This will create two authorizations which will be evaluated independently of each other

# Question 30: Transaction code access

We have a user that is able to run every transaction code. I've checked the profile in SU01 (not SAP_ALL) and all the roles for this user, but I couldn't locate the tcode. How can I find the error?

**A:** Has a manual profile been given to that user? You may find the authorization for the tcode in there. If not, use SUIM to filter out your selection.
Look in UST04 to see what profiles the user has. There may be a strange entry for a tcode object in UST10C in the field BIS.
Run Report RSUSR060 (where used - for auth values). Then search for obj S_TCODE for a value of all transactions '*' by profile.

Your user should be assigned to one of these.

# Question 31: Authorization object V_VBAK_VKO

How can I create a customized table for data maintenance allowing access only for user controlled by sales area level using authorization object V_VBAK_VKO?
We won't give SM30 to the user, so I have created a new tcode for the customized table.

**A:** You have a few options:

Create a customized program.
Use parameterized tcode to table (see tcode OB52 as an example). It only controls the auth group you add to the table through SE11, SUCU or SE54.

Create the customized program and add S_TABU_LIN configuration to control access to a field in the table.

# Question 32: Accidental authorization objects

Inadvertently, we created a handful of custom auth objects that we did not want in SAP_ALL. They were added automatically; how can I remove them?

**A:** Maintain the profiles in the profile generator Tx PFCG. Use SM30 to maintain PRGN_CUST. Add entry: ADD_ALL_CUST_OBJECTS. Blank is the default value = 'YES'; change it to 'NO'.

# Question 33: Tracking user data

How do we track data being accessed by a specific user? (i.e., we need to know who is accessing, viewing or maintaining, certain employee payroll data.) Is there a log report for this?

**A:** HR data access can be seen via the change document reports in HR; viewing may be impossible.

ST03 and STAT will tell you what reports and what SE16 tables were accessed.

# Question 34: Changing user defaults

How can allow a central user to change user defaults and parameters for other users without allowing full-access to SU01? We currently authorize users to change their own settings with SU50 and SU2, but we haven't figured out a way to do this without opening up access to maintain user roles and profiles, which we do not allow.

**A:** You can do this by allowing access to SU01, but not giving S_USER_AGR or S_USER_PRO. That way no roles or profiles can be assigned, but all other data can be maintained (name, address, email etc). You can further limit what user groups access is granted for via S_USER_GRP. This may cause issues in a productive environment; test thoroughly before executing.

S_TCODE <OBJ> Authorization check for transaction start
TCD <FLD> Transaction code
SU01
S_USER_GRP <OBJ> User Master Maintenance: User Groups
ACTVT <FLD> Activity
02
03
CLASS <FLD> User group in user master maintenance

# Question 35: Changing authorization group names

I need to change the authorization group names for a large number of tables. What should I protect against when doing that? I plan to work in DEV boxes, transport to QA and to live.

**A:** Make sure your roles are adjusted to the new auth grp values before the changes go live. Users probably won't even notice. You can use some tables in your preparation: Table TDDAT can be used to see all the tables that have a certain auth group.

Table TBRG for object S_TABU_DIS will give you all the auth grps allocated to a table controlled by this object.

Tables and their auth group can be seen in tcode SE54 and SUCU as well. Table TBRG only has the "documented auth groups." You can use what you want and they do not have to be in the table TBRG

# Question 36: Authorizing hierarchies

Is it possible to authorize hierarchies in transaction code UCMON in SEM-BW? I need to prevent the display of the entire hierarchy when a user is not authorized for it. I can authorize the activities, but users can see the entire tree/subtree of all hierarchies that have been created.

**A:** If your users are only displaying data, they should do it in bex analyzer, which prevents them from viewing the consolidation monitor. Bex is the ideal mode for controlling the level of hierarchy.

# Question 37: BDC user vs. service user

What is the difference between BDC user and service user?

**A:** A BDC user is one designed to be used for a BDC session (batch input session) run in batch. A few places SAP check the type of user before it allows the process to complete. SM35 is one; its password does not expire and it cannot be used interactively.

Communication ID is designed to be used in RFC connection defined in SM59. The password does not expire and the id cannot be used in dialog processes.

A BDC user ID can be used in SM59 RFC but a Communication ID (CPIC) cannot be used in a BDC session.

# Question 38: RESPAREA

Previously, RESPAREA has been made an org-level. When viewing the object in the org-level it shows that there is access to HI, KN, KS, PC and PH.

Our customer is having a problem in KO04. A trace shows that it fails on RESPAREA with OR in K_ORDER. When looking at RESPAREA in the object itself I can see OR as an option, but not in the org-level.

How can I include OR in RESPAREA in the org-level?

**A:** Try Note 565436.

# Question 39: HR go-live

We are preparing for an HR go-live with structural authorization applied. We have the following business requirement:
A user has 1 centralized OM and PA display roles (the whole organization). This user will also need a PA admin role that we have created, with a structural profile that limits access to a specific ORG unit.

If I assign all three roles to this user, the result is that he will have the combined access of all three roles, however he will only be able to view the entire ORG through his OM and PA display roles because the structural profile will restrict him to the single ORG unit overall.

Is there any way to have structural profiles apply differently for each role?

My goal is to allow this user to view the entire ORG via his OM and PA display roles and maintain (i.e., PA30) only specified ORG units via a PA Admin role and structural restriction.

**A:** In standard SAP probably not. There is a change you can use in the function module option on the structural authorization to get it to do what you want. The other option, if you are in the correct version, is to look at the new objects in HR, called contexts, that allow you to assign the PD profile to the authorization (role) and it may accomplish what you want.

One other check is to see if the org management tcodes check object P_ABAP, (use ST01 authorization trace). If it does you can make it program specific so it bypasses the other checks for that program only.
The context solution works well but is only applicable to PA and not OM (i.e. no context for OM related objects).

The P_ABAP solution only switches off infotype checks, not structural auths, and only for reporting of items running through logical databases SAPDBPNP/ SAPDBPAP.

There is a document on service.sap.com, called "context sensitive realization of the authorization check in HR master data" which covers functionality. It should solve most of your issues, depending on how complicated your system is.

# Question 40: Field values in auth groups

I have a Essential regarding authorization groups. When we give field values for authorization objects have a field named authorization groups, (i.e., in object mm_mate_wgr, a field for authorization group is given).
How can we create these authorization groups? Is there a tcode or another way to do it?

**A:** You don't have to create the field codes, but you can if you want. You can enter an arbitrary 4 character string and as long as it matches with the one you have put on the corresponding data set then it will work.

If you want to know how to set them up so you will get a drop down list, run a search to get a few detailed posts about the steps you need to take.
M_MATE_WGR

Enter something in the authorisation group field in the basic data material master view.

Give users access to the auth group in their role for this M_MATE_WGR object.

# Question 41: CCMS Configuration

I get a logon error.which reads: Logon failed; Call of URL
http://<xi-system>:8000/sap/bc/bsp/sap/spi
monitor/monitor.do terminated due to error in logon data.

**A:** First, check the validity of your SSO ticket for this system. If you do not have a user ID, contact your system administrator.

Error Code: ICF-LE-http-c:100-l:E-T:21-C:3-U:5-P:5-L:7

HTTP 401 - Unauthorized

If the user ID and password are correct; it may be an authorization issue.

If you are using 6.40 WAS, double-check your input. In the higher releases, passwords are case sensitive for non-ABAP to ABAP.

# Question 42: FICO SME

I have a FICO SME attempting to set the Auth Group in the above object to a specific value, say 0001 for display only and he negative tested and put in the value in the testid of 0002 and it passed when it should have failed. He did the SU53 but got the "successful auth check" message. This should not have happened according to our security field settings.
The SME is attempting to restrict users to particular auth groups when displaying report groups. Again this does not seem to work. When he adds a group to the auth group for the G_801K_GLB object, it allows access. I ran a trace and it is not even checking the object. The object is checked but not check maintain. How can we resolve?

**A:** You may have found a technically empty shell concept and you will need to look for a different control object. Your last resort is S_PROGRAM; but you will need a concept first.
It's possible that you're expecting the object to work in a way it is not intended. The object controls who can change the layout, not use it. There should be another set of G_xxx that are used to control use of the layout. If the auth group is blank, (it is not showing up in the trace) see if the documentation in SU21 for the object can help.

# Question 43: Self-service password reset

Is there a self-service tool with which end-users can reset their passwords themselves? I imagine a function call with a web surface would be quite effective. Does anyone have some code/tool to sell?

**A:** The Standard Tool should allow for user authentication against LDAP/RACF password, determine if user is locked or not in SAP (and if administrator locked - disallow unlock), reset password and send email to user with new password.

# Question 44: Transaction VF02

I want to prevent users releasing billing documents to accounting in transaction VF02. The activity to release is 43, but this activity is not assigned to the authorization objects for this transaction.

**A:** Open the activity selection screen for a given authorization object.

Left click > Select "More Values"

All activities as listed in table TACT will appear for selection. If you are still having problems, hit the F7 key on your keyboard in the Activity dialog box - this will show all available ACTVT values, regardless of whether they relate to the object.

# Question 45: Remote copy

We did a remote client copy from PRD (Source) to DEV (Target) selecting SAP_USER profile.

The remote copy was successful but we are unable to see the basic maintenance and complete views in the target client's PFCG transaction. Are there any settings that can get both?

**A:** In transaction PFCG, go to the top menu bar. Under utilities there is an option for the view you need.

# Question 46: Surveying departments

We are in the implementation phase of SAP, and I have been assigned the task to taking a survey and notating the users in all departments (modules) for our SAP User Licenses.

What is the easiest way to prepare user lists? (It was very difficult to get an overview of users.)

**A:** Create user groups to categorize the users with transaction SUGR. This makes for simple reporting through SUIM.

**Note**: Use USMM to display current license classifications and assign accordingly.

# Question 47: Op SAP PS

We have set op SAP PS for use in two company codes/plants. We want to set authorizations in such a way that staff in one cc cannot write time on networks in the other cc, but so far have not been able to find a solution for this.
We are using CATS for time writing and have 2 separate WBS structures in each cc, with some WBS elements in cc A to a project in cc B.

We want to ensure that people in cc A do not write time on networks in cc B.

**A:** Are you referring to CATS and not performing scheduling on the projects? If it's CATS limitations you're looking for, you would need to explore the CATS user exits. Test carefully; CATS is very temperamental and you are potentially impacting a large number of users that would be/could be attempting to charge to a project.

Exit to consider:
CATS0006 CATS: Validate entire time sheet

If you're looking at limiting network restrictions within PS functionality, use:
CNEX0002
EXIT_SAPLCNAU_003 PS Customer Exit Network Header Auth Check
EXIT_SAPLCNAU_004 PS Customer Exit Network Activity Auth Check

These same exits can be called from non-PS transactions, particularly PM, since networks are a form of order (shared by PM, QM, CO ....). Again, know what you're doing and test carefully.
By activating these exits, and not even adding code, you'll find you've brought the logistics modules to a stand still until you've added at least one line of code to them for SAP_X_ACTVT - returning a value of 'X'.

# Question 48: Transaction execution

Is there a way I can find out which transactions a particular user used on a certain day?

**A:** Use STAT for up to 24 +/- hours; ST03 or ST03N for up to a week. After that, it gets summarized to weekly and monthly data.

# Question 49: Auth object f_lfa1_grp

Can auth object f_lfa1_grp be used in TRANSACTION level?

It works in XK01/FK01 (create vendor) but not in FV60/F-43.

**A:** This is a master data control object. Use authorization groups and F_BKPF_BEK to have group specific control at the transaction level.

# Question 50: Query group in QuickViewer

We have secured SAP queries based on Query Group. However, when a query is created using QuickViewer, then converted to a SAP query for use by others, it encounters an authorization failure because the user does not have S_TABU_DIS display access for the authorization group of the underlying table. Without knowing every query in the query group and every table assigned to the query group, how do we give access to this query?

**A:** There is no way without analyzing each Quick Viewer and each table it uses and then referencing TDDAT table for the auth groups.

If you use PFCG's option to "add a report" (as opposed to "add a transaction") and have PFCG create the transaction code, you will not need to use the user groups at all.

You can configure SU24 with the tcode PFCG creates to all the S_TABU_DIS requirements, so when the tcode is added to any role you will not have to recreate the access each time.

Some prefer to avoid user groups for queries by adding the generated report (not the query) to a report tree or role, which helps avoid all the user group pitfalls.

# Question 51: Critical combinations

Is there a report in SAP that can show all the critical combinations of transactions assigned to a user? (I tried a report in SUIM but it needs the table SUKRI to access the list of critical combinations.) Is there another route to finding a list of the possible critical combinations?

**A:** You can run RSUSR008 for tcode combination but it will not tell you if the user can complete the tcodes.

RSUSR009 can be configured to show conflicting access based on the authorizations needed to complete the business processes. In higher versions there is a RSUSR008_009_NEW that allows you to define business processes so the results are easier to determine.

A few matrices have been posted in the forums over the last couple of years - you may want to search for these.

You could get some generic info from these sites:

http://www.auditnet.org/ - you may need to register.

http://www.sapbasis.org/securitydocs.htm

Note: Prior to running these programs, determine what your company considers "critical" or you will yield a great deal of work for extraneous information.

# Question 52: Creating a role in SAP CRM

I am creating a role in SAP CRM with transaction PPOCA_CRM : Creation of New org unit.

Once I add the transaction to the role, I can't see transaction code but get Description "Create org Model" instead. How can I view the codes from the role which were added?

**A:** In the menu part of the role, there is a + sign; click on that and you will see transaction + description.

# Question 53: Specialized login problems

I am not able to login into PRD server using SAP* login and DDIC login. I also tried with default password of these ids also. (06071992,19920706,PASS). Our seniors set the password for these ids and were later resigned. I am not able to find the original passwords.

Some experts in this site told to execute the below query and try to login again:

Before executing the 'Delete sapr3.usro2 where bname = 'sap*' and mandt = '122';', I want to run the select query for this.

While executing the following query in OS level, I get the error message: "table or view does not exist."

pmldev:devadm 1>sqlplus /nolog

SQL>connect /as sysdba;

Connected.

SQL>select bname from sapr3.usro2 where bname = 'sap*' and mandt = '122';

select bname from sapr3.usro2 where bname = 'sap*' and mandt = '122'

*

ERROR at line 1:

ORA-00942: table or view does not exist

SQL>

**A:** If this system was installed with version 4.7, you must use a schema owner:

Select bname from sap[SID].usro2 where bname = 'sap*' and mandt = '122';

# Question 54: Executing ST03

I am attempting to execute ST03 and am unable to find the usage history in enterprise version. Once I execute, I do not know how to proceed.

**A:** Use SE11 to understand what ST03 used, then use SE11 again to help yourself to find what is new /changing.

# Question 55: Turning off modify data

I would like to recommend our BASIS person turn off the modify data value of variables during debug mode in our production system to avoid accidental direct debugging table updates and integrity problems.
How can we implement this security profile so that it can only be given to certain individuals?

**A:** Debug with replace S_DEVELOP activity (ACTVT) = 02 and OTYPE = 'DEBUG' - all other fields are blank (represented by single-quote-space-single-quote)
You can also update debug with 03 in older releases/ level if you can submit a program in update task.
You can also globally deactivate normal debugging in higher releases via a control of the debugger session from the dispatcher. You will get a message stating "Debugging is impossible at the moment - Please try again later."

# Question 56: Cross module roles

I have a problem with a user who is working in both HR and EHS, so needs a cross module combination of roles.

We have created a custom auth object for P_ORGIN for the HR roles and it is working the way it should.

However, when we combine the EHS with the HR role, the user is missing IT0002 for all subtypes. We want this user restricted to Subtype 9 in the HR role but want the user to view all subtypes in EHS transactions.

Currently the user can only view the users who are in subtype 9 in any of the EHS transactions. Is there a way around this?

When we give the user access to IT0002 for all subtypes, the EHS transactions show all employees and all the HR transactions the user is also able to see all employees which should not happen. The user should only see employees who are in subtype 9 in PA20/PA30.

**A:** Try OSS Note: 508254 EHS-IHS Authorization check for HR data.

# Question 57: Role FBL3N

I have created a role with FBL3N as its sole transaction and limited it to an authorization group "AA" for GL accounts.
I have added an entry to TBRG for auth obj F_SKA1_BES and given it a value of "AA." I have also changed one GL account to have an auth group of "AA."

However, when I logon as my new user with the FBL3N role, I cannot see the GL account line items for the account that has been given "AA."

I know that the FBL3N role is working because I can see other accounts which have no auth group attached.

**A:** Run a ST01 authorization trace. Manually add authorization group F_BKPF_BES into the role and limit it to "AA." Add this entry to TBRG and everything should work.

# Question 58: Object F_IT_ALV

What is the benefit of object F_IT_ALV? I am interested in activity 70 (administer) and would like know what it does exactly and what access does the user get if the activity is set to 70?

**A:** Activity 70 gives users the ability to administer layouts in transactions like FBL1N & FBL3N. This should be restricted to prevent users altering layouts used by other users.

(From the Help Text): Object F_IT_ALV controls the availability of functions for layout maintenance in the ALV list for the line item display. This authorization is optional. If it has not been maintained for a user, it does not affect previous functions. That is, all layout functions are still available without restrictions.

Defined fields
Object F_IT_ALV has a field, activity ACTVT, that can have one of four values: 01, 02, 03 and 70. Each of the activities 01, 02 and 70 specifically controls the availability of a function (in the menu or application toolbar) in the ALV line item list:
01: "Settings -> Display variant -> Save"
02: "Settings -> Display variant -> Current .." and
"Settings -> Display variant -> Current header items"
70: "Settings -> Display variant -> Administration"

Activity 03 is the minimum, most restricted authorization: The user can only select preconfigured layouts. All other functions are inactive for activity 03.

If, for example, you want a user to be able to change the column selection and the header items and save this new layout, but do not want him to administrate the layout, then you would give this user authorization for activities 01 and 02.

For more information, see note 374656.

# Question 59: Transaction PV7I

We have an employee trying to book a training from transaction PV7I by pressing "Request Attendance." The system has the message "You have no authorization for the function or the object." When I check the SU53 it said "All authorization checks have so far been successful."
Are there any other tools to prove that this user is authorized or is their some other way to circumvent?

**A:** On rare occasions, SAP performs a simulation of authorization checks. Thus, no SU53 is present but the user is not authorized. In some cases the error message is wrong.

**Note**: Try debugging the code and breakpoint a message to find where and what is causing the failure.

# Question 60: Building roles in PFCG

When I want to build a role in PFCG, how can I exclude objects like IS-Beverage and IS-Real Estate objects from appearing in PFCG? Is it in SU22 or SU24?

**A:** You can exclude an authorization object via SU22/4.

It is recommended to "inactivate" the object in a given role.

# Question 61: Management roles

Change management for roles when I go to SUIM - change documents - roles the values for "old value" and "new value" are blanks.
This is the case for many roles.
Why is the change management for roles not activated?

**A:** Set the "from date" to a date in the past and select "All Change Documents (Technical View)".

## Question 62: User comparison

Is there any way that the user comparison can be automated? Currently, we manually compare the roles. I have heard that a parameter change will do the trick.

**A:** Use transaction code SUIM > Comparisons > From Users

Note: Schedule RHAUTUPD_NEW to run periodically.

## Question 63: List personnel areas

Is there is a table, program or a transaction code to run for a list of personnel areas that have been created for HR?

**A:** Try table T500P

# Question 64: Transaction codes FSoo/FSPo

Our supervisors have requested that transaction codes FSoo (G/L Account) and FSPo (G/L Account in chart of accts) be made display only. This would not be a problem as I could set the Activity to 03.

However, they need users to create and change access to transaction FSSo which uses the same objects as FSoo and FSPo. Do you know of any way to make the above two transaction codes display only?

Is there a way to assign another display only object to these transactions that would not be checked by FSSo?

**A:** It is best to give transactions a standard display only tcode and separate the roles.
Reconsider your design and challenge the requirement by changing the tcode. Your company should not request tcodes, but rather a requirement. Give them something to click on and it does not matter what it is called.
You can change the auth checks a little bit with Se93 (at start) and using SU24 check indicators. Hardcoded checks, if reacted to, are the only real checks.
Use the authorization concept to grant auths, depending on whether you want to achieve display or change. Generally, you activate 03 or 02.
Solution may be a combination of both: "What did SAP check?" AND "what did the user have?" (Sometimes the "How did SAP react to the check?" also plays a role.)

# Question 65: Assigned role in child system

How do I find what role I assigned to a user in the child system? I ran report "display change documents for role administration" via transaction SU01 but it only shows the roles of the CUA system.

**A:** Just go into the target (child) system and use the table AGR_USERS.
SE16 -> AGR_USERS
Change the "From date" in "Change Documents for Role Assignment" from the current date to a date in the past.
Or, from SU01, you can select "Change Documents for Users."
The report will show you the deleted profiles.
The above report with table AGR_PROF will allow you to see the relation between a profile and a role. There are few steps involved, but this will provide you the wanted result.

# Question 66: Db-tab TCURR

Our users must be authorized to change entries in the db-tab TCURR.
We are in SPRO; what do I have to do to authorize?

**A:** TCURR is maintained via tx OB08. You need to restrict this + change access to S_TABU_DIS auth group FC32.

## Question 67: Executable transactions

How do we find out the executable transactions within multiple roles at one time?

**A:** Put them all in a user id and execute transx RSUSR010.

Note: In lower versions, RSUSR010 may not warrant the results you need, but in higher versions it will tell you if the user has S_TCODE and the auth object tied to the tcode defined in SE93. It will not tell you if the user can complete the tcode or if the user has access to run a business function executed by a CALL TRANSACTION within another tcode.

RSUSR009 (or the new one), configured correctly, can provide you a more accurate result.

## Question 68: PHAP_SEARCH_PA

I restrict employee access by creating a personnel area role. However, when user executes transaction PHAP_SEARCH_PA the report generates a list of data from the entire personnel base. What is wrong? Could it be the report doesn't have an authorization check through Query?

**A:** Run a ST01 authorization check to see what has been checked. If the report is based on a Logical Data Base it may be checking P_ABAP which overrides the P_ORGIN check.

## Question 69: Restrict Report Variant access

How can I restrict access to edit the Report Variant of others? Is it possible?

**A:** Yes, when you go to save the variant, click the box that says "Protect Variant." Once the field Protect Variant is selected, it can only be changed by the person who created or last changed it.

**Note:** If a user has access to report RSVARENT, they may be able to access and/or modify the report.

## Question 70: Overwrite user authorizations

I have created a few users with a set of authorization and roles. These users' names are already in use. I would like to overwrite the authorization of the users by copying roles and profiles of another user without deleting the existing users.

**A:** Remove the existing roles in SU01 and replace with those you want to want to copy from the access form.

# Question 71: Restrict ME21

We want to restrict tcodes ME21n based on Item Category , but there is no object where we can specify item category field value. We tried to set the trace , the it does not show any object that has item category as field for any object

Users can select item type inside the tcode me21n. What can be done to restrict based on the item category?

**A:** You can include additional authorization check in the ABAP (User Exit).
Steps:
Search for an already existing authorization object, which might fit.
If such an authorization object does not exist, create a customized authorization object.
Include the authorization object into a User Exit.
Assign the authorization object to the transaction via SU24.
Regenerate the impacted role in expert mode.

## Question 72: Content repository

I am trying to create and configure a Content Repository (transaction OAC0) so I can use my own Content Server with ArchiveLink. When I try to save my configuration, I get the message, "User DDIC may not make changes in Customer systems."

**A:** Try another i.d. and the user a_ch2005 without SAP_ALL.

You are getting this message because the DDIC user has limited create & change access in SAP.

You should not use DDIC for these tasks.

However, DDIC is required for certain installation and setup tasks in the system, so you should not delete it.

## Question 73: Download list of all SAP transactions

How can I run a report to generate a list of all SAP transactions? I know I can view a list from SE93 and SM01, but I need to download a full list.

**A:** Try table TSTC for a list of transactions. The texts are in TSTCT.

# Question 74: Finding tables

I have assigned roles to positions. What tables is this data held in?

**A:** There is a relationship in IT1001. Try table HRT1001 (it may be or in conjunction with HRP1001).

In older versions, it is IT1016

 In 4.6C, we use HRP1001.

Object type = S
Rel.Obj.Type = AG
ID Rel.Obj = your role name

You can play with the other fields (end date, etc) if needed.

# Question 75: User authorizations

I need to provide authorization for read only of a database table and to other users read and inset/update rights.

What type of user authorizations do I need to build into the code?

**A:** If you want to restrict the tables in SE12/16/17, you can do that via an authorization group: Assign group to the table and use the authorization object S_TABU_DIS. Coding shouldn't be required.

If you want to provide the authorization access via a program: Use a transaction table to be populated through the program.

Note: Only users with specific access/authorization should populate it.

SM30 (Or create a tcode in SE93 and call SM30 with skipscreen option); Use S_TABU_DIS to search values (see SU21).

Activity 03 = display
Activity 02 = change (etc.)

Use S_TABU_DIS (tode SUCU) to DESIGN what you want to achieve.
Use SU24 / PFCG etc to CONTROL it.

# Question 76: Security - Material Master

Is it possible to restrict people to changing/creating the standard text in the basic data view (or any other views) within the material master?

**A:** Yes, it is possible. It can be controlled by clicking on Views> m_mat*.

# Question 77: Super-user authority for emergencies

We need to have the ability to grant super-user access to support users in case of emergency system maintenance.

The technical part we can handle. How can we install a good process to track and control who gets this access & when?

**A:** Emergency Access within individual organizations depends on a number of factors, the major one being who decides there is an emergency & who authorizes this access.

When the issue is raised there should be a person like a senior project person or a team responsible for classifying issue as emergency. What a user perceives as emergency is often in the grand scheme of things not that critical. This needs to be ratified by someone with good "high level" view of what's going on.

On making the decision, the decision maker should e-mail the person responsible for granting this access with a completed form (this can be completed retroactively) stating that emergency access should be granted for reason x to user y. This may seem an unnecessary step, but ensures a non-SAP audit trail for the decision making process & ensures there is accountability down the line.

Adding the access to a support user for a limited amount of time and adding the role for 1 day only in the UMR is probably the best idea as it ensures there is system evidence for that made what changes & when. If you have the Security Audit Log switched on, this can help, otherwise you'll have to trail through the single stat records.

When the user has finished then they should inform the process manager they have finished so the access is removed and the form updated with the completion of the job.

It's a bit rough and ready but will give you a bit of an overview of the processes to go through. I can't stress too much the

importance of getting a project manager or similar to approve the action before it takes place!
After all precautions have been taken, you have two options in accomplishing your objective.

First option is to assign the role to the user and the change documents in SUIM will show when the user was assigned the access and when it was deleted STAT or ST03 will tell you what they did.

Option two is to create an emergency ID and unlock and lock to control access to the ID.

# Question 78: CUA for R/3, BW. APO

I need to implement CUA for R/3, BW and APO.

My question is, is it possible to implement it for these three (3) modules, using one central system?

If yes, then which system should be the central system?

Also, we are having a three (3) system landscape for R/3, APO and BW.

**A:** CUA is often set up via a workplace shell linked to all SAP systems. CUA is useful without single sign on as it can make user admin easier, especially if you have many clients.

However, I don't think it's worth the effort unless you need single sign on if you have just R/3, BW & APO & limited clients per system. CUA on the surface is a good idea, but be very sure you need it before setting it up as the time saving benefits for performing an action that can be wasted by doing something else more efficiently.

# Question 79: Authorization of VA02

The sale order is make-to-order with configuration. How do I configure the authorization to be as follows?

The user has the authorization VA02 to change the sales order, but the user will have no authorization to use the menu EXTRA----CONFIGURATION to modify the material configuration in the sales order change screen.

**A:** Try to switch on the check indicator for transaction VA02 and authobject C_TCLA_BKA in transaction SU24. Make sure that you do no grant permission to that object.

This will work only, if the same user is not required to access configuration elsewhere. If so, maybe you need to switch the same auth object for the "elsewhere" transaction.

# Question 80: Authorization

I have some questions concerning authorization. I would like to know which one you think is better: Outsource Authorization to a consulting company or keep the authorization in house.

Is it worth tje money to take a consultant to help develop authorization concept?

Do you use SAP predefined profiles, use them and edit them or do you use only custom-developed profiles?

**A:** There are a lot of ways to approach your queries, but before that let me point out some other important concepts on security and authorizations:

An authorization is only a component of providing a secure & controlled SAP environment. If you lack the skills in house to develop a secure solution with business controls appropriate to your business then it is worth paying an outside organization to manage this. This also depends on the size of rollout, future scalability & company policy.
As with all other areas of SAP, a decent consultant/contractor will be able to design/help you design a solution that addresses security, segregation and business process controls within a manageable framework.

Regardless of the route you want to take, it is important to speak to your internal audit department as they can be good allies when things get tough & can offer good advice on this subject.

Personally I would not advocate outsourcing the whole security operation. Get a contractor/consultant to come in and work with an employee dedicated to the task. Preferably the employee is someone with knowledge of the business, not someone who has "done a bit" of security on AS400 etc. Ensure knowledge transfer takes place and you will be in a good position to maintain & expand the solution going forward.

If you already outsource functions like Basis, IT infrastructure or Application Support then it may be easier in the long run to get the supplier to do this work as well.
3. Another option is custom developed roles. This allows you to create user access based on your business processes & requirements, not those specified by SAP. In some cases the SAP standard roles can be useful guides i.e. admin roles. If the role built is based on business processes defined by the process teams & approved by whoever is looking after SOD etc., you will end up with roles that mainly reflect the business requirements.

A word of precaution though, if you do decide to get consultants for the job, make sure that your consultants will require good functional security plans and help meet those needs while maintaining the desired security level. I have been on projects where security was an after thought or the functional groups were not required to provide their requirements. In the end a lot or work had to be redone and there were many unhappy users in the process.

An experience consultant that knows how to ensure no segregation of duties are present in roles and who can deliver you a simple easily understood security structure can be invaluable. One that says they know it but actually do not will cost you more in the long run.

## Question 81: Restricting access to certain fields in VA43 / VA03

Is it possible through authorizations to restrict a user from displaying certain fields within a sales order or contract etc.?

I thought that it was possible to create field groups in configuration and then to restrict who accesses field groups via the profile, in a similar way to how the object F_KNA1_AEN works in XD02.

**A:** What you are saying is possible but not as delivered by SAP. Field level control is only applicable for MASTER data, not to transaction data. The Vendor, Customer, General ledger and Credit management master data should be allowed field control, and no other place based on standard security measures.

# Question 82: AR - Creating customer master data

I want to restrict the creation of customer master data for a user to a specific account group type that we have created. We are working in 4.5B.

Is this possible?

**A:** Look to see if auth object F_KNA1_GRP is available. If not you will have to configure authorization group to be mandatory.

If F_KNA1_GRP is there, SAP may not be checking it if the value is blank. If so Account group must be made mandatory.

Just a tip – the account group is not controlled by field status. It is always mandatory as it determines the number range and field status of the customer master record. The problem with using it for authorizations is that it is only checked in the master record maintenance. To control postings, the authorization group has to be used as mentioned above in conjunction with F_BKPF_BED.

# Question 83: Get possible values for customer authorization group

We are going to be using the customer authorization group (KNA1-BEGRU) for authorization objects F_KNA1_BED and F_BKPF_BED.

At present the users can enter any value allowed by their authorization profile but if they make a typo, they get an error. We want to prevent that from happening.

Where do we maintain the values for the drop-down?

**A:** It sounds like the match code help is not configured for this.

Some of the auth groups are stored in table TBRG with the key being the auth object. Try entering it there to see if it shows up.

The table has to be modified for the screen to enable it to be a dropdown.

# Question 84: Authorizations for settings

Which authorizations (settings) are not allowing any changes in the application server?

We are on NT-4.0 OS, Oracle-8i DB and 40B application environment.

**A:** If you are talking about locking the system for changes, try transaction SCC4.

In addition to SCC4 you may have to look at se03 system change options as well.

# Question 85: CATT

Is there any way to control the CATT script by authorization?

**A:** In principle, yes there is because you could write your own function module to check. This function module may be called by function "FUN" in CATT and then by using function "IF" (or similar).

There are some disadvantages of ABAP coding though. Creating or executing CATT scripts through transaction code SCAT requires authorization object S_DEVELOP, and in that object you can limit access as you want, as this object carries fields such as activity, dev class, object name, etc.

# Question 86: A list of all PM transactions - 46C

We want to compile a transaction / role matrix and I only have an outdated list of PM transactions.

How can I get an updated list?

Is it possible to get the description of the associated profile to also pull through to align alongside the transaction?

**A:** Here's what you need to do:

1) Create a dummy activity group.
2) Add the full tree of PM of the SAP standard menu.
3) Generate the authorization profile.
4) Lookup table AGR_1251, restricted to your activity group and object S_TCODE.
5) Pick up the value in column LOW.

If you need the description as well, also do the following:

1) Load the result from above into xls.
2) Load table TSTCT into xls.
3) Use xls function LOOKUP() to bring it together.

For your last question, the answer is yes, there is a way. There is another table AGR* giving the transaction codes together with descriptions. You could simply do a search while online to give you the appropriate table numbers.

# Question 87: Authorizations - Transaction CAT2

Within transaction CAT2, I have restricted the transaction to allow users to be able to update their own records only and an administrator to be able to update all. I also need to allow a user to be able to update a group of users.

What is the best way of doing this as the organizational menu is not configured yet?

They need the ability to update other records for users belonging to the same "Time Admin Group".

**A:** Try to have a look at the object P_ORGXX, with this object you should be able to control access based on the Time Data Administrator.

Before you use it, remember to activate it (T-Code OOAC) first.

# Question 88: Profiles deleted

I have to give a user some profiles for a limited number of days. Is there a timestamp feature that could just assign the profile for three (3) days or so and then delete the profile automatically?

If so, how do we do that?

Please take note that I don't want to delete the user together with the profile.

**A:** If you created the profile manually then there is no time stamp. To let the user access a profile for a limited amount of time you need to do the following:

1. Create an activity group and generate the profile via the profile generator PFCG.

2. Assign the user this activity group in his/her master record and here you can input the "valid to date" the last date you want the user to access the profile.

I am assuming you run "mass compare" on daily basis as a batch job. This tool will remove the profile from the user master record hence he/she can not access the transactions contained in this profile after that date specified in the "valid to".

Do mass comparison by running transaction PFUD or report RHAUTUPD_NEW.

# Question 89: Transaction Report - Roles

Does anyone know if SAP provides a report to list all transactions maintained in a role (for 4.6C)?

I don't need the info for just one role; I need it for all the custom roles we created.

**A:** If you have a naming convention for the profiles for the custom roles then you can use table UST12.

Do the following:

Enter S_TCODE for the Object/OBJCT field
Enter you profile name i.e. Z* in the authorisation/AUTH field

This will very quickly tell you all the transactions that users have access to. These won't necessarily appear in their menu, but will be available if they use the transaction fast entry box.

Alternatively you could use table AGR_1251:

Role/AGR_NAME Z* etc
Object/OBJECT S_TCODE

Take note, this is a "quick & easy" method of finding T_CODES within a role, but is potentially not as accurate as using UST12, especially if not all the roles are generated.

It may also be worth looking at table AGR_TCODES. Like before, it's potentially not 100% accurate, but it provides a "quick & easy" solution.

The above options will yield semi accurate data but SUIM is based on the USTxx tables which get out of sync with the real tables USRxx. AGR_TCODES only shows what is in the menu not in authorization. For object S_TCODE AGR_1251, it only shows what can be in access and not what actually is. PFCG is only a temporary info sheet that has no

meaning until you hit generate, so if a role was "saved" and not generated the real access is not reflected in the AGR_xx tables. UST12 is a text table that gets out of sync with the real Security tables.
You can run the Sync function module in mode 'X' to increase the accuracy but it can generate an error and add more access to the user than the role originally had if you do not have the latest path.

So if you want the get a 100% accurate answer you will have to use tcode OPF0 (it looks like SU01) and the menu path INFORMATION-OVERVIEW-USER or Authorization or profile. The only quirk is that the entries in the fields are case sensitive.

You can also try this transaction: S_BCE_68001425 - Roles by Complex Selection Criteria .

# Question 90: Tracing security authorizations in BEX Analyzer

We are running SAP BW 3.oB. A user attempts to process a query in BEX analyzer and is not able to successfully access the query. No authorization error message is displayed to the user.

We have attempted to trace the user's authorizations with ST01 and RSSM with no success.

Is there another way to trace or list the user's authorizations while they are in BEX?

**A:** Yes. Use RSSMQ for query instead.

# Question 91: Authorization object for a t-code

I have not done any work on authorizations for a very long time and I have forgotten everything on CA940.

I am giving some users access to a transaction. How can I find out which authorization objects affect a particular t-code? I entered the t-code in S_TCODE fine and I just need to find the authorization objects for it.

**A:** Use profile generator t-code PFCG and everything taken cared of for you if you enter the t-code in the menu.

You can look at what is configured for each t-code in t-code SU24.

## Question 92: Restriction on personnel number within CAT2

Does anyone know if it is possible to restrict access like display/change to user's own personnel number inside CAT2?

Does ESS use object P-PERNR?

How does this work?

**A:** You're right with the P_PERNR. To the field PSIGN give value 'I' and remember to check you have Communication info type 0105 subtype 0001 maintained for the user (with the user-id).

## Question 93: SM35 guidelines

How do I handle SM35?

Which actions should not be allowed? Is there a handy way to restrict use for own batch inputs only?

For maintenance, does it make sense to use field BDCGROUPID?

The numbers of roles are expected to grow.

**A:** First of all, you can give only S_BDC_MONI (ANAL , ABTC). Don't give S_BDC_MONI (DEL).

# Question 94: Profiles for super user

How can you look for profiles for sap*?

How can we make a user, a SUPER USER?

Is sap* considered a super user?

**A:** If you want to make a user a SUPER USER, you need to assign the user SAP_ALL and SAP_NEW profiles in SU01 transaction.

Usually SAP* is hard coded in SAP Programs and yes, SAP* is a super user. You can disable SAP* account by setting a profile parameter.

SAP* is only hard coded from the standpoint of what it cannot do, and not what it can do in the higher versions of SAP. SAP* , as long as it is defined in SU01, is a super user ONLY if the ID has SAP_ALL attached, if any other access is granted it can only do what it is allowed to by the roles attached. It has no Special Access unless you delete it in SU01.

Any user can be a SUPER USER by assigning SAP_ALL, in higher versions of SAP SAP_NEW is not needed as SAP_ALL is generated using RSUSR4xx programs or in SU21.

# Question 95: KE5Z Company Code restrictions on Profit Center line items

I am trying to restrict on company codes for KE5Z, so that the users can only display Profit Centre posting for their own company code. As it seems in 4.6c the Comp. Code check is not performed and they can display all profit centers with line items created in other company codes.

Does any one have any experience with this?

Obviously this can be fixed through an ABAP re-coding, is there an easier way of doing it?

**A:** SU24 displays all the check objects in a transaction, KE5Z shows that company can be checked, you need to switch check/maintain on and that will automatically bring the company code check object into your activity group. If you fail this, manually add it in.

Have a look at auth object K_PCA field RESPAREA. There you can give values for the profit centers.

Furthermore, if you are in Profit center accounting where Company code has little meaning, you will have to control the Profit center as indicated above.

# Question 96: Retrieve authorization profiles for specific company code

How do I retrieve all profiles/roles by company code?

**A:** Having a good naming convention helps a lot in the retrieval process.

You can go into table AGR_1252 and in the Company Code and that will bring up every role with that company code assuming you are not using ranges.

# Question 97: Restricting access by organizational unit

Although this is not my subject area, I've been asked to find out if it is possible to restrict users by organizational unit. For example, a user can only see information pertaining to a specific plant, though there may be many plants in the organization. Our Basis people have had little success in sorting out this problem.

How can I achieve this?

**A:** You can create copies from the roles you are using. Then assign the needed plants. This authorization object is located under the tab "organizational levels". Finally, assign the role to an user id t-code pfcg.

Organizational levels, like plants, help control SAP authorizations at a very fundamental level.

Just execute report RSUSR040 & type *plant* as the Authorization Object Text to get an idea of the objects.

Your Basis / Security Administrators should attend a SAP Security course to better implement/design a security plan.

Alternatively, if you maintained all organizational levels from the organizational level window in the authority tab of PFCG, do a table dump of AGR_1252 on $WERKS. The field is case sensitive.

# Question 98: Auth in Transaction sm12

I need for a user to view locked entries but not delete.

Is this possible?  How can this be accomplished?


**A:** Yes it is possible.

SM12 uses auth S_ENQUE. Take out the Standard value * and put in DPFU.
This should only allow display and not the ability to delete the lock. Test it to make sure you are happy with it.

# Question 99: General concept - CUA + security best practice

This is a general background question.

Working with new dimension plus CUA with a workplace, we have a normal implementation of GCR'S, TDD'S and BPP'S.

What are some of the best practice ideas that I should keep in mind when building profiles?

Here are some specific areas:

- Is one transaction per BPP the best practice? If so, why?
- What are the types of profiles I need?
- What are naming conventions?
- How do I build up the parent child relationships?
- Are there any bugs in CUA I should know of?

**A:** Here are some things to ponder:

1. One (1) transaction per BPP is highly recommended. It keeps it simple. It is easy to track during the build & it keeps your documentation tidy. Each transaction should be linked to a process & the functional team completes the documentation for that process. It also helps when you are unit testing your transactions. 1 BPP = 1 transaction keeps it modular & flexible.

2. Types of profiles? You should end up with groupings of BPPs that relate to activities within the organization like performing month end closing of accounts. Your GCR should form a role that contains a number of activities to represent what the end user needs to do. Try and avoid your final role/GCR from being a composite role in SAP. They are a pain to maintain & although they save time during a build in the long run they often cause more problems than they solve.

3. When designing the naming convention, look at the following identifiers - regional, module i.e. MM, SD if you are using modular based build system like SEM, R3, variant info & brief descriptor. You need to decide if you are going to use a profile

generator long names or stick to naming convention that will allow identification of profile as well as role.

4. About parent and child. Make sure that you need this. If you are ONLY restricting by organizational data then it is alright to use. However, if any of your variants are going to require field level security or different transactions then don't bother with Parent-child hierarchies, they will cause more problems than they will solve. If you decide that the transaction inheritance feature is too good to resist when using field level security, you should take great care that field changes are not overwritten by someone hitting the "generate from parent" button.

When you build your roles, trace every transaction & make sure USOBT is kept up to date via SU24. There will be cases where there are unnecessary authorization objects & value pulled through which can give extra access. There will also be many cases where the authorizations pulled through are insufficient. If any authorizations values e.g. activities need to be changed and have "changed" status, these need to be fixed via SU24 & avoid any "manual" entries if possible. These measures will slow your build up initially, but will make the system far easier to maintain going forward.

# Question 100: Transfer authorizations and roles of a user to another

I am trying to copy/transfer a user authorization to another one. I know I can re-create it by copying that user to another. But I have already created the user and would like to have the same rights.

Is there an easy way to do it?

**A:** Yes there is. You will probably have to ctrl+y and cut and paste the authorizations. A good tip is not to do this from the UMR as the table will not scroll down to include all of them, run a report from sum and you will be able to cut the whole lot into an Excel sheet and then paste it in 10 or so at a time into the UMR of the target.

# Question 101: When to reset the User Buffer

When do I reset the user buffer.SAP asks to execute the function module SUSR_USER_BUFER_AFTER_CHAGE.

Are there any consequences in resetting User Buffer?

**A:** You can reset it when you know a user has the proper access assigned and still, they are still receiving errors. Then check THE ENTIRE SU53 output and if in someplace it shows "does not exist in user buffer". That is the only time to reset buffers. It does not happen that often and there are no exact reasons why it happens.

I use report RSUSR405 and it doesn't have any negative consequences likw hosing up user access while they are logged on or degradation of system performance. It works like a gem.

# Question 102: Background jobs (SA38)

If I have a user authorized for SA38 how can I stop him to setup an unauthorized background using a "super" user to gain access to unauthorized transactions?

**A:** If a user has got SA38 access they also need to have SUBMIT / BTCSUBMIT for the authorization group the program is assigned to. This is done via S_PROGRAM authorization object.

They will not be able to use other user's authorization to run a program via SA38.

To ensure the user cannot run under another's ID you will have to remove S_BATCH_NAM from the user. Also Removing BTCSUBMIT from the user's access will only stop the user from running the reports that have an authorization group on the Report (SE38 Attributes screen). If the Report does not have an authorization group the report will run without any check. You maintain authorization groups on reports using RSCSAUTH report.

## Question 103: Keep or transport Favorites on another system

A lot of our users have customized their favorites and have done a lot of transactions with modifications of the designation.

Is it possible to transport a "favorite" on another system? If yes, where does the system stock the user's favorite.

**A:** I don't think it's possible to transport favorites. What you can do is use the SAP Easy Access Menu Download and Upload and then upload your favorites to your pc.

The alternative is quite a long process. See the following:

Code:

```
REPORT ZEXPORTFAV .

tables: smen_buffc.

datA: begin of t_fav occurs o.
      include structure smen_buffc.
datA: end of t_fav.

select * from smen_buffc
  into table t_fav
  where uname = sy-uname.

CALL FUNCTION 'WS_DOWNLOAD'
    EXPORTING
        FILENAME        = 'C:sapfav.txt'
        FILETYPE        = 'DAT'
    TABLES
        DATA_TAB        = t_fav
    EXCEPTIONS
        FILE_OPEN_ERROR    = 1
        FILE_WRITE_ERROR   = 2
        INVALID_FILESIZE   = 3
        INVALID_TYPE       = 4
        NO_BATCH           = 5
```

```
        UNKNOWN_ERROR        = 6
        INVALID_TABLE_WIDTH  = 7
        GUI_REFUSE_FILETRANSFER = 8
        CUSTOMER_ERROR       = 9
        OTHERS            = 10.

IF SY-SUBRC <> 0.
* Enter you error handling if needed.
ENDIF.
```

************

```
REPORT ZIMPORTFAV .

tables: smen_buffc.

datA: begin of t_fav occurs 0.
      include structure smen_buffc.
datA: end of t_fav.

CALL FUNCTION 'WS_UPLOAD'
    EXPORTING
        FILENAME          = 'C:sapfav.txt'
        FILETYPE          = 'DAT'
    TABLES
        DATA_TAB          = t_fav
    EXCEPTIONS
        CONVERSION_ERROR     = 1
        FILE_OPEN_ERROR      = 2
        FILE_READ_ERROR      = 3
        INVALID_TYPE      = 4
        NO_BATCH          = 5
        UNKNOWN_ERROR        = 6
        INVALID_TABLE_WIDTH  = 7
        GUI_REFUSE_FILETRANSFER = 8
        CUSTOMER_ERROR       = 9
        OTHERS            = 10.

IF SY-SUBRC = 0.

* ADD SECURITY AUTHORIZATIONS HERE IF NEEDED

  delete from smen_buffc where uname = sy-uname.
```

commit work and wait.

loop at t_fav.
  insert into smen_buffc values t_fav.
endloop.

commit work.

For another alternative:

Tables SMEN_BUFFC and SMEN_BUFFI

1) SMEN_BUFFC - gives information of all storing Favorites per User; the name of the included transaction code is available in the REPORT field of the SMEN_BUFFC table.

2) SMEN_BUFFI - gives information about all Links for Favorites per User; you will see the Web address if you double click on a row of the table.

# Question 104: user master compare

What's the best way to assign users to roles in 4.6C? I have been using PFCG to assign users to roles, but have been warned that the user master compare can cause users to lose authorizations and that roles should be added to the user master in SU01. I know that profiles should not be generated in the Production system but are there any dangers in pressing the user master compare button?

**A:** You can use any method you like. You just need to know the consequences of the actions you choose. Roles can be assigned either through PFCG or SU01. PFCG is best used when you need to assign many users to one role; SU01 is best used when you need to assign many roles to one user.

The "save" in SU01 performs the same codes as the save in PFCG. Note that the jumping from role tab to profile tab and back can cause profiles to "disappear" if a role-profile is assigned without the role.

The user master compare looks at the from-to dates and adds or removes the access based on those date. it also removed role-profiles when the role is not assigned. It will also look at the HR role assignment and adjust accordingly.

Note that the from-to date means nothing to SAP unless you run user compare or PFUD.

So for those losing access the system is doing exactly what is asked of it, and generally, the user is not aware of what it is asking.

# Question 105: Display Authorization for Customization

Is there any role provided by SAP for Display authorization of complete IMG? Should I give this role in the production environment to Functional Experts?

How can I create roles of Display authorization of IMG for different modules? By this, I mean Display IMG authorization of QM, Display IMG auth for SD and other such functions?

**A:** You do not really need a "functional expert" for this. You can create one in PFCG if you have projects defined in the IMG or you can download the list of t-codes from the IMG and upload them into a menu in PFCG and generate the authorizations, this however will create a configuration role. You will then have to create a new role and insert the objects from the "do" role and then change all the values to display one (activity 03), note though activities are more than field ACTVT.

As long as it is 100% in display and your system settings are correct, then you cannot configure in production with this role. The tables for the list of t-codes are another matter though – it is a cus_actobj.

If you create a project for each of the modules in the IMG you can then create role specific for each module in PFCG. However many modules overlap so they will not be pure.

# Question 106: Profile Deletion because of Role Mass Comparison

Something very strange happened in our 4.6C system.

We have a user called PAT which was created for special printing software. This user has no role but directly a composite profile assigned which includes 2 profiles: 1. Y1 and Y2. These profiles are not assigned or connected to any role.

When we execute a mass comparison of ROLES Y* and Z*, this comparison causes that one of the profiles Y1 is not only removed from the user PAT but deleted in the system. Y2 stays in the system, stays in the composite profile and stays assigned to the user.

Why did that happen or why did a ROLE comparison touch a role-independent profile?

**A:** The user compares reconciling roles & profiles within UMR's though this is not exactly how the process occurs. If no role is found within the UMR, any profiles could be seen as being left over from roles & would be deleted as there is no link to a role. It's reasons like this that it helps to avoid role and profile based access within a system.

I am not sure why the UMR is deleted though. I bet the profile is not deleted from the system. Most likely you are searching for it using the wrong name. Remember it this way, when a profile is created with PFCG it actually has two names, one name for the MENU (role) and one name for the generated profile. Some administrators use longer names for the role (menu) so they can identify it by the naming convention more information about why the profile was created. The generated profile portion (the collection of authorizations) will have a 10 digit name. If the admin that created the profile gave it the exact same name when the profile was first generated at creation time as he did the activity group (role) at creation time then it is a little easier to do searches for the profile. However what often happens is that you have a generated profile with the name ZF>XXX_XX_ and the Role is named ZF>XXX_XXX so when you go to PFCG and look for you missing profile you might be entering ZF>XXX_XX_ which is what you remembered seeing in the profile tab section before you ran the user master compare report. It may be that the ZF>XXX_XXX is still there. Use PFCG and ZF>X* and find all similarly named profiles and you might find the slight difference in the name of the Role versus the Underlying Generated Profile.

As you have learned by this you cannot assign a generated profile directly to the profile tab section of SU01. A warning message will appear if you try and remind you that if there is no corresponding Activity Group / Role when the user compare runs it will delete the generated profile from the user.

Therefore NEVER assign generated profiles directly, but assign the Role instead. The exception to this is that if you have a composite profile that was created with SU02 and these profiles in the composite profile are generated profiles (they were created with PFCG) you can assign the SU02 created Composite Profile to the profile section of SU01 for the user and they will not be "cleaned" out when you run a user compare report.

Not that you would want to use SU02 composite profiles but this time, it will work.

# Question 107: Urgent - Authorization

There are a lot of company codes for instance. Can I restrict users to view only those selected through the F4 drop down help?

I have defined in organization levels, access to company code 999 but when I drop down help, I can see everything.

**A:** If you are on release 4, you can use a search-help exit to perform an authority-check, and delete lines that fail. Take a look at the online help for Search-Helps, and also the template function module:

F4IF_SHLP_EXIT_EXAMPLE.

For example, search-help H_T001 is attached to the data element BUKRS, so you could add the search-help exit here (it involves a repair).

To add authority-checks to the Company Code field:

Using SE11, edit the search-help H_T001. In the search-help exit field, enter Z_H_T001_SHLP_EXIT (or similar).

Take a copy (named as above) of function module F4IF_SHLP_EXIT, ensuring that you include the statement TYPE-POOLS SHLP in the Global Data area.

In the section for CALLCONTROL-STEP = 'DISP', you need to add code that will extract the Company Code field from RECORD_TAB, perform the appropriate authority-check, and then delete the record if the check fails. Putting a break-point in here is useful for seeing the format of RECORD_TAB, as it has no structure.

# Question 108: Authorization for field BLART

Is there any way of limiting the access of a user by document type in transaction Fb-02?

We want a user to be able to enter in the books only one type of document at a time.

**A:** You will have to put an authorization group on the document type master records in order for SAP to begin checking the authorization for document type. Except for table maintenance, SAP does not perform the authorization check if the value of the Authorization group is BLANK.

# Question 109: Standard Menu and User Menu Options

Isn't there a parameter for having the system default to the Standard menu?

What I mean is that if the user has an activity group (role) and they login, they will see their user menu, if they select the standard menu icon and logout, the next time they log in they will see the standard menu.

I know how to turn off user menus.

Is there a parameter that ignores what they were viewing last and always defaults to user menu?

I am getting information here and there about the different options, from changing the SSM_CUST to user individual based start up options.

It would be nice if all these were collected in one place such as an OSS note on Standard Menu vs. User Menu options. I have only been reading them for two days so maybe I am not being patient enough with my notes search.

**A:** No, there is no parameter.

There is a configuration setting in SSM_CUST table the values I believe are:

ALL_USER_MENUS_OFF
CUSTOMER_MENU_OFF
SAP_MENU_OFF

# Question 110: Updating Organizational Levels in Profile Generator

I have a lot of Activity Groups where fields that can be maintained at Organizational level have actually been maintained manually at Authorization level. The result of this is that a subsequent change to the field at Organizational level does not make the corresponding change at Authorization level.

How can this be reset? For example, for a given activity group I need to be able to change all fields that are for WERKS via the Organization level, regardless of whether they have been manually maintained.

The system release is 3.1I.

**A:** Yes, you can reset the organization level with the ABAP AGR_RESET_ORG_LEVELS. The result is that the organization levels in the authorization objects of a role are reset to the value that you enter for the entire role with the button "Organization level". Unfortunately you can only run it for one role at a time, maybe a CATT could help if you have to reset multiple roles. Hope that this ABAP exists in 3.1I as well.

AGR_RESET_ORG_LEVELS is only applicable to 4.5+ in 3.1 you are hoses and have to look in the appropriate HRT1251 table to find the key, but you will have to go in an update each role. The authorizations are probably in the "changed" state.

# Question 111: Authorization in transaction SA38

How do I give authorization to execute all programs except RPUDEL20?

I tried without success: BC_C: *
S_PROGRAM: A* - RPUDEL19
RPUDEL21 - Z*

I tried many different combinations but didn't find the appropriate way to do it.

How can I do this right?

**A:** You can assign an authorization group to the program. That way it should not execute unless the user has the authorization group assigned to them within a role (auth s_program, field p_group).

There is a program that allows you to assign authorization groups to programs/reports. It's RSCSAUTH but I recommend you trawl through to posts as I'm not 100% certain.

Putting in the program names in s_program won't work as there are two (2) fields p_action which allows the action to be performed i.e. execute, submit. p_group is the authorization group.

RPUDEL20 isn't even allocated to an authorization group by default in most if not all versions.

The long term solution could be done as follows:

1. Do not grant SA38/SE38 in Production.
2. Assign transaction codes to all ABAPs that end users would need to execute and include them into roles/build roles for them.

There is good news though. Most of the standard end user reports are already assigned to transaction codes (S_ALR*, S_BCE*, etc.).

The problem with restricting on authorization group level is that it is quite difficult to restrict separate programs as you wanted it. With the approach above it is much easier, because when excluding SA38/SE38 you would just not grant the t-code which is assigned to the specific program.

Of course administrators will shout and cry when you take SA38 away from them because some need it for basis administration. These could be exceptions.

# Question 112: Authorization for testing

I want to give end users the authorization to see but not change the configuration. Also they should be having front-end transaction to carry on with the testing.

How can I achieve this?

**A:** You could grant objects:

S_TABU_DIS with Activity 03 Display and auth.group 0*-O*, Q*-Z*
S_TCODE with SPRO. You will probably also need other customizing transactions as O* (O like in Omega), AO* and SM30.
S_TABU_RFC with activity 03 Display to enable customizing comparison to other systems
S_PROJECT with activity 03 Display and * in the rest

But be careful. T-codes O* in combination with S_TABU_DIS activity 02 of another role that a user might have can lead to table change authorizations that are of course not intended in Production.

# Question 113: SAP_ALL Dilemma

We are contemplating on giving an administrator the responsibility of creating new users. However, if they can create new users, what is there to stop them from creating a user with SAP_ALL authorization for themselves?

**A:** In SU01 object s_user_pro you can specify the profile names that the user has access to. If you have a profile naming convention you can enter the relevant ranges here. If you use SAP Standard profile names you can use t-* etc.
You also need the process in place to monitor these things.

While the S_USER_PRO and S_USER_AGR is the proper TECHNICAL way of controlling the assignment of SAP_ALL it does not prohibit them from assigning enough Customer developed roles and profiles to create a SAP_ALL equivalent ID. Therefore it is incumbent, as part of the supervisor's responsibility, to review the work being done by monitoring what the person is doing. This is done with the Change document reports. So limiting the access to one role is not sufficient.

# Question 114: Authorization for entry only thru program

How do I restrict a user to pass a document only via an ABAP Program and prevent him from passing the document thru the transaction screen?

If the authorization for the transaction is removed, the program fails and if the authorization is given, the user can't be prevented from passing the entry externally.

How do I make this work?

**A:** You are using BDC session. From there, use function module BDC_OPEN_GROUP to create a session into which the BDC_INSERT can be used to insert batch input data.

The syntax for the function (excluding exceptions) is:

Code:
```
CALL FUNCTION 'BDC_OPEN_GROUP'

        EXPORTING  CLIENT      = VALUE
                   GROUP       = VALUE
                   HOLDDATE    = VALUE
                   KEEP        = VALUE
                   USER    = USER FOR AUTH CHECK
```

The great thing about this function is that you can specify the user for the authorization check. If you specify a dedicated background user with the relevant authorizations, the job will run well as all the code performed within the session will use the authorizations of the user specified. Therefore the user doesn't need the authorizations for the sensitive transaction.

Security requirements should be included where applicable within the functional specs of any custom ABAP, but this is often overlooked.

It is poor design for functional teams to make workaround to suit the developers unless there are no other options.

In versions prior to 4.6 this was not a problem since the CALL TRANSACTION function bypassed the S_TCODE check. In 4.6 you have to go into transaction code SE97 and tell SAP NOT to check on a CALL TRANSACTION. You do have to be at a very high patch level since some programmers HARD CODED the S_TCODE check in some of SAP's T-codes which bypasses the SE97 feature.

As suggested above creating a BDC session to run rather than a "direct" call transaction is also a good approach. If you want the Document to be tied to the user who ran it though you will have to run the BDC session under the ID the of the requesting user and not the segregate the user.

Still the use running the "transaction" will need the underlying authorizations, so while they may not be able to run a specific t-code they may be able to accomplish the same through another set of screen for a t-code that they do have.

A point to note is that the user id to check authorizations has to be passed even with the SUBMIT command or else the authorization will fail. Also one drawback is that the environment parameters do not get set in the current session and therefore to retrieve the same, one has to necessarily access the database tables which may prove to be time-consuming.

# Question 115: Mass Deletion of Roles

Is there a way to delete bunch of roles?

**A:** Yes there is. But you have to use Debug to do it.

In SE38 run program
AGR_DELETE_ALL_ACTIVITY_GROUPS, run in Debug mode,
enter in the AGR's you want to delete, when you get to these
commands:
CALL FUNCTION 'PRGN_CHECK_SYSTEM_TYPE'
EXCEPTIONS
SAP_SYSTEM = 1
OTHERS = 2.

IF SY-SUBRC <> 1. EXIT. ENDIF.

You need to change SY-SUBRC to equal 1. This tells the program
that it is a SAP AG system, which in turn will let the program
continue.

You have the choice of deleting the roles by using Modules or
directly from tables.

It is better to set-up a Macro using Modules.

There is also SAP note 313587 regarding Mass Deletion of Roles.

Alternatively, use T-code SCAT and record PFCG with delete
option of a role. Then find the field from the test case and create
a parameter for that. Export default variant. Then edit this file by
entering the roles you want to delete. Finally execute the test case
with the variant file. This works well.

# Question 116: Role in CUA and DEV Client

In our Company, CUA is created in the workplace machine. We have two (2) Development Client. My questions are:

1. How can I transfer a role from DEV Client (A) to DEV Client (B)?

2. Is it necessary to transfer the role to CUA (i.e. WP machine)?

**A:** If your roles are on the same system but different systems, you can transfer the roles a couple of ways:

1. Download via PFCG & Upload into new client. Use the SCC1 and cross client copy. Put your roles into a transport request in client A. Don't release it and use SCC1 in the target client (B) to import the transport.

If I have to do this & the other development client isn't in the standard transport path, then this is the process I will use. Usually I will request that the different development clients that require up to date roles are included on the transport path.

2. If you are going to be using CUA from WP, then the roles will have to be read into WP. If you have a role in a CUA'd system that hasn't been read into WP + text compare etc. you won't be able to use CUA to assign that particular role to a user as WP won't contain the link to the role.

# Question 117: CAT2 (Timesheet) again: object P_PERNR

I want to restrict users on changing only their timesheets. I want it to be as follows:

1. The parameter PERNR in transaction OOAC is already set to 1.
2. two HR master records have user IDs assigned in info type 0105, subtype 0000.

Restriction "I" in the field P_PERNR-PSIGN does not work, the test user can still change/display timesheets of all users. But Restriction "E" in the field P_PERNR-PSIGN works meaning a user can maintain all timesheets except his.

Is there something specific on how I should enter the "I" value (I like in Investment)?

**A:** After setting OOAC, make sure you set P_PERNR as C/M for CAT2 in SU24. If you do this and you are still having problem you could trace CAT2 to see if it is picking up P_PERNR. If it doesn't then there may be some more configurations to do.

I believe it is Info type 0105 subtype 0001, and not subtype 0000, In version 4.6 SAP indicates it uses IT 0105 subtype 0001 instead of the t513A entry. Check table T77ua as well.

P_PERNR does not work exactly like documented but the 'I' is to indicate Individual only, and 'E' is basically useless.

Try switching P_ORGIN to inactive in your role - this should then work. If this works maybe set back to C (check) in su24.

An alternative would be to deactivate P_ORGIN with change authorizations and grant display for P_ORGIN only, then I already can restrict the CAT2 change authorizations to the own personnel number only (by granting P_PERNR with value "I" in field Psign and info type 0316).

# Question 118: T-code specified display

Our internal auditors used a t-code at one time to generate a report or screen that would display a given t-code, the user(s) who are authorized, and the activity they have authorization for example, display or change.

Does anyone know of such a t-code?

**A:** You could check the RSUSR* - reports.

It is RSUSR010 that shows you the transactions of a user and when double-clicking on the transaction, it shows also the activities. The t-code to execute that report would be S_BCE_68001429. Usually all these reports start with S_BCE*.

# Question 119: FB02 - Document change

We want to restrict some users from removing the block payment from certain documents within a vendor. All the security objects that restrict block/unblock seem to be at the master data level i.e. vendors. We do not want to block the vendor from payment but various documents within a particular vendor. In transaction FB02 and FB09 the field for block/unblock is available to be changed. We want this enabled for the finance people but not for anyone else. One option is a transaction variant, but I wonder if there is an object I missed or configure that an application specialist could do?

**A:** I could imagine that the authorization objects in connection with invoice verification (transactions MR02, MRBR) would control if the user can only make normal changes as the text or release MM invoices.

You can check the authorization objects M_RECH_* of the objects class MM_R.

## Question 120: Generate activity group in Production client

I've been changing some authorizations in an activity group that we give to our application developers. When I transported it to pre-production from development, they lost access to lots of transactions. I solved this by regenerating the profile. The same problem has now occurred when the activity group was transported to production.

We run an overnight batch job to generate all profiles which completed successfully, and other activity groups that were transported were fine. I wonder if the problem may be due to having full authorization in object s_t-code as this was the one that wasn't being read to the user buffer.

Is this usual?

**A:** Yes, I've seen it before. Just let that user re-login to the system again.

You could also try a mass-comparison (run program PFCG_TIME_DEPENDENCY in background). We usually schedule that as job once per night.

# Question 121: PFUD

We have expired multiple users from an activity group and after running pfud it deletes the generated profile from the su01 for said users but the activity group (role) still exists in the role tab. Is there a way to delete this also without having to go into pfcg and delete users from the ag? My assumption was that pfud did this but in fact it only deletes the profile.

**A:** If the profile is not in the user buffer, the user will not have the access given by the expired activity group, so it does no harm to leave it in there.

Or you can try function SUSR_SYNC_USER_TABLES
Use value X.

You can also use the user exit in the PFCG/SU01 save routines to remove the entry of expired roles. PFUD and Syncs will not do it. The exits are configured in SSM_CUST table.

The SSM_CUST entries are:

ID Path
Z_EXIT_USERS_SAVE =
ZSEC_USER_COMPARE_COMPLETE
Z_SINGLE_USERPROF =
ZSEC_USER_COMPARE_COMPLETE
Z_USERS_TRANSFER =
ZSEC_USER_COMPARE_COMPLETE_TAB

THe function module call a a bit different for each
ZSEC_USER_COMPARE_COMPLETE is format
CALL FUNCTION 'ZSEC_USER_COMPARE_COMPLETE'
Exporting
Activity_group = Activity_group.

In the function module you should delete the entries in AGR_USERS where the To-date is less than the current date "sy-datum".

for

ZSEC_USER_COMPARE_COMPLETE_TAB
The call is
CALL FUNCTION 'ZSEC_USER_COMPARE_COMPLETE_TAB'
Tables
ACTIVITY_GROUPS = OK_TABLE.
Note: this exit sends the records that have changed in an internal table, however if nothing has changed the table is empty.
Therefore the user ID is retrieved from the calling program and the Roles are then processed based on the Userid.

# Question 122: MEDRUCK - Put 1 part delivery schedule per 1 site

I have to modify MEDRUCK form. My task is to put DELIVERY Forecast on a printout. Currently ZMEDRUCK (copy of medruck) prints data in the following way:

Quote:

Material1 Week no. Delivery qty.

\-------------------------------------------

42 100

: :

52 120

Material2 Week no. Delivery qty.

\-------------------------------------------

42 10

: :

52 20

My problem is I have to make sure 1 material schedule is printed on 1 side. Page break can not occur within a schedule, but there could be more schedules within 1 page.

Example:

Schedule is not longer then 15 weeks. I could adjust window size to 15 weeks, but if there is a zero quantity in a week the line is not printed out, hence the first line from the next item (in such case - header line) is printed out on the 1st page, and the rest of it on the 2nd page.

How do I solve the problem?

**A:** You have to specify page-break protection in the print program around those sections where you don't want page-breaks to occur.

CALL FUNCTION 'CONTROL_FORM'
EXPORTING

COMMAND = 'PROTECT'.
and

CALL FUNCTION 'CONTROL_FORM'
EXPORTING
COMMAND = 'ENDPROTECT'.

This is to respectively start and stop page-break protection.

# Question 123: MK01 Create Vendor - remove change rights to payment

I have found a way how to restrict MK01 Create vendor in order to prevent changing General datA: Payment Transactions. Users are allowed to change all but not the bank details.

How do I define and assign field authorization groups to vendor master.

**A:** In SPRO go to Financial Accounting --> Accounts Payable and Receivable and from there to Master Records. Create "Field Group"´ + define fields into created field group.

It is that simple. Create a field group and assign that two digits group number to object F_KNA1_AEN. In field group you define the fields you do not want to be edited (f.ex LFA1-BANK ect).

You might need help from an abaper in order to find the field names. Field name can be found by pressing F1 on the field and then "technical info".

# Question 124: BEx No Authorization Problem

I have a strange BW BEx problem. I created an activity group and was testing it in the BEx. When the workbook loads and refreshes I get a "no authorization" error. When I run the trace, all authorization checks are successful. When I use my ID and execute the workbook in BEx all authorization checks are also successful but the workbook executes without errors. I have never had a trace not identify the authorization problem.

How do I resolve this?

**A:** Authorization checks on BW don't show up in ST01. Using RSSM the authorization check log can give extra object authorization i.e. show what is checked and you can compare it to what you have got. One problem is that you can't run the trace on your ID; you will have to copy your access to another ID and use your ID switch on to trace for them.

SAP Standard Auth checks will turn up in ST01, but any custom object you have created through RSSM and have assigned to a Cube will not.

# Question 125: PAYROLL SECURITY

What is the best way to restrict access to Audit reports by Info Type?

I have entered Authorization Object P_ABAP.

**A:** This report rpuaudoo call FM HR_CHECK_AUTHORITY_INFTY.

So it's check P_ORGIN.

# Index

"changed" state............... 101
"high level" view...............62
"super" user ....................90
*plant* ............................84
40B application
    environment................ 71
ABAP Authority check .....22
ABAP coding..................... 71
ABAP re-coding................82
ability to delete.................85
access ....9, 12, 16, 17, 18, 20,
    22, 23, 25, 26, 27, 28, 31,
    32, 33, 35, 40, 41, 45, 47,
    52, 53, 54, 56, 58, 60, 62,
    63, 65, 67, 71, 74, 75, 76,
    77, 78, 81, 88, 89, 90, 94,
    98, 105, 107, 114, 115, 120
access configuration.........65
Activity Groups............... 101
administrator 34, 36, 74, 105
APO ........................11, 12, 64
AR - Creating customer
    master data .................69
assign . 12, 32, 37, 52, 63, 75,
    81, 84, 94, 97, 102, 109,
    119
Assigned role ....................53
Auth in Transaction sm12 85
Authorization.. 14, 16, 17, 18,
    19, 20, 23, 25, 27, 28, 29,
    32, 33, 34, 36, 39, 40, 45,
    46, 47, 49, 50, 52, 54, 55,
    56, 57, 60, 65, 66, 69, 70,
    71, 73, 77, 78, 83, 84, 87,
    90, 95, 99, 101, 102, 103,
    104, 105, 106, 107, 112,
    113, 119, 120, 121
authorization check log.. 120
Authorization for entry .. 106
Authorization for field
    BLART ..........................99
authorization for testing 104
authorization group .. 23, 29,
    33, 40, 46, 60, 69, 90, 99,
    102, 103
authorization group names
    .....................................29
authorization in house..... 66
Authorization in transaction
    SA38 .......................... 102
authorization objects . 16, 17,
    19, 20, 25, 27, 33, 36, 70,
    78, 87, 101, 113
Authorization of VA02..... 65
Authorization reports ...... 18
Authorizations -
    Transaction CAT2 ....... 74
Authorizations for settings
    .....................................71
Authorizing hierarchies ... 29
Background jobs (SA38)..90
basic data view .................61
basis administration ...... 103
batch input data ............. 106
batch inputs....................80
BDC session.......31, 106, 107
BDC user...........................31
BEX Analyzer ................... 78
BEx No Authorization
    Problem..................... 120
billing blocks ................... 22
block payment.................113
BPP'S ..............................86
CAT2 ........... 74, 80, 110, 111
CAT2 (Timesheet) again.110
CATT................... 24, 71, 101
CATT script ......................71
CCMS..............................34
Changing doc types.......... 24
check indicator for
    transaction.................. 65
classifying....................... 62

combinations ...... 16, 41, 102
company codes.....38, 82, 98
compile..............................73
composite profile ....... 96, 97
composite role ................ 86
configuration role ........... 95
configure authorization
  group........................... 69
Conflicting combinations.16
consequences .......88, 89, 94
Content repository........... 58
control10, 26, 35, 39, 44, 62,
  63, 68, 69, 71, 74, 82, 84,
  113
critical...........................41, 62
critical combinations........41
cross client copy.............109
Cross module roles ......... 45
CUA .............53, 64, 86, 109
CUA + security................ 86
CUA for R/3, BW. APO ... 64
Cube..............................120
custom developed roles....67
custom roles.....................76
custom-developed profiles
  .................................... 66
customer authorization
  group........................... 70
customized ......25, 26, 57, 91
DDIC.......................... 43, 58
deactivate ................44, 110
Debug ..................15, 44, 108
debug mode.................... 44
dedicated background user
  ..................................106
degradation of system
  performance ............... 89
DELIVERY Forecast....... 117
desired security level.......67
Development Client........109
Disable SPRO.................. 23
disappear....................... 94

Display Authorization for
  Customization.............95
document type.................99
DPFU ............................85
dropdown........................70
dummy activity group......73
Emergency Access...........62
emergency ID .................63
end users................103, 104
entire role ...................... 101
Executable transactions...54
execute ....24, 43, 44, 54, 84,
  88, 96, 102, 103, 108, 112,
  120
Expert mode .................... 19
expired multiple users ....115
expired roles ...................115
extra access.....................87
F_IT_ALV ......................47
fast entry box ..................76
FB02 - Document change
  ...................................113
FBL1N ............................47
field group.....................119
Field level control.............68
Field values.....................33
from-to dates ..................94
front-end transaction.....104
FS00...............................52
FSP0..............................52
full authorization............114
full tree..........................73
function "IF"................... 71
function module ..32, 71, 88,
  98, 106, 115, 116
Functional Experts..........95
functional specs............ 107
functional team ..............86
fundamental level..........84
future scalability..............66
GCR'S ............................86
generate ...58, 75, 77, 87, 95,
  112, 114

Generate activity group...114
generated profile .96, 97, 115
Global Data area..............98
good functional security
    plans ............................67
good naming convention .83
grant.....52, 62, 65, 103, 104,
    110
grant permission ..............65
HR 16, 27, 32, 33, 45, 51, 94,
    110, 121
HR and EHS .....................45
HR master records ......... 110
ID switch.........................120
identifiers..........................87
in house.............................66
individual based ..............100
internal auditors..............112
internal table ...................116
invoice verification..........113
ITAR................................. 21
KE5Z ................................82
KE5Z Company Code
    restrictions ..................82
knowledge transfer...........67
limited clients ..................64
limiting the access ....99, 105
link .....................18, 96, 109
locked entries ...................85
locking the system............ 71
login problems..................43
lose authorizations ...........94
Macro .............................108
maintained manually ..... 101
Management roles............50
mandatory ................. 20, 69
manually add ....................82
mass compare...................75
Mass Deletion of Roles ..108
mass-comparison .............114
MASTER data..................68
master data level .............113

master record maintenance
    ....................................... 69
master records ................ 99
match code help ..............70
material master......... 33, 61
ME21................................ 57
ME21n ............................. 57
MEDRUCK......................117
MK01 Create Vendor ......119
mode 'X'........................... 77
modifications ..............21, 91
modify data .....................44
modular ......................86, 87
modular based build system
    ....................................... 87
monitor....14, 21, 30, 34, 105
month end closing ...........86
Movement types.............. 18
multiple roles ............54, 101
naming convention9, 76, 87,
    96
negative consequences ....89
new dimension.................86
no segregation of duties... 67
non-SAP audit trail ..........62
NT-4.0 OS .......................71
numbers of roles ..............80
OAC0 ..............................58
object P_PERNR.............110
object P-PERNR..............80
one central system ..........64
one role...12, 24, 76, 94, 101,
    105
Oracle-8i DB ....................71
Org Level Tables ..............17
organization levels ... 98, 101
organizational levels ........84
organizational menu........ 74
organizational unit...........84
outdated list .................... 73
outside organization ........66
Outsource Authorization . 66
outsourcing ......................66

overnight batch job......... 114
P_PERNR.........80, 110, 111
page-break protection ... 117, 118
parameter PERNR.......... 110
Parameters tab.................16
password ........ 31, 34, 36, 43
PAYROLL SECURITY .... 121
personnel areas.................51
personnel number .... 80, 111
PFCG  20, 27, 37, 40, 50, 60, 75, 77, 84, 94, 95, 96, 97, 108, 109, 114, 115
PFUD................... 75, 94, 115
PHAP_SEARCH_PA....... 54
PM transactions - 46C......73
possible values ................. 70
pre-production................ 114
Production client ........... 114
profile based access ......... 96
Profile Deletion................ 96
profile generator .. 13, 27, 75, 79, 87
profile generator t-code PFCG...........................79
profile naming convention .....................................105
profile parameter..............81
Profiles deleted .................75
Profiles for super user ......81
profiles/roles.................... 83
Profit center accounting.. 82
Profit Center line items ... 82
Profit Centre posting ....... 82
proper access assigned .... 88
PSIGN give value 'I' ......... 80
PV7I..................................... 49
Query group .................... 40
ranges .............................. 83
release ..15, 36, 98, 101, 109, 113
relevant ranges ...............105
re-login ........................... 114

Remote copy ..................... 37
report RSUSR405 ............89
report scheduling ............. 14
reset the User Buffer ....... 88
RESPAREA................ 31, 82
restrict.17, 18, 21, 23, 32, 35, 53, 54, 56, 57, 60, 61, 68, 69, 80, 82, 84, 98, 103, 106, 110, 111, 113, 119, 121
restrict access23, 56, 80, 121
Restrict Report Variant....56
restricted roles.................. 14
restricted the transaction.74
Restricting access 23, 68, 84
Restricting access from MM03............................23
retrieval process ...............83
Retrieve authorization profiles...........................83
Role . 9, 10, 12, 17, 19, 20, 21, 24, 32, 33, 40, 42, 45, 46, 50, 52, 53, 54, 57, 59, 62, 63, 67, 73, 76, 77, 83, 84, 86, 87, 94, 95, 96, 97, 100, 101, 104, 108, 109, 110, 115
role assignments............... 12
ROLE comparison............96
Role Mass Comparison ....96
role matrix ........................73
role specific......................95
role-profile .......................94
roles of a user .................. 88
rollout ..............................66
RSCSAUTH report ..........90
RSSMQ .............................78
RSUSR008 ....................... 41
RSUSR010 ..................54, 112
RSUSR060......................25
RSVARENT.......................56
S_BCE*......................103, 112
S_TABU_DIS 17, 29, 40, 53, 60, 104

S_TCODE 20, 25, 28, 54, 73, 76, 77, 78, 104, 107
SA38 access ..................... 90
sale order ......................... 65
SAP AG system .............. 108
SAP CRM ......................... 42
SAP Easy Access Menu Download and Upload. 91
SAP predefined profiles ... 66
SAP Standard Auth ........ 120
sap* ........................... 43, 81
SAP* account .................... 81
SAP_ALL 25, 27, 58, 81, 105
SAP_ALL Dilemma ........ 105
save ... 47, 56, 58, 87, 94, 115
SDP94 ............................. 12
seo3 system change options ..................................... 71
SE11 ............... 17, 26, 44, 98
SE93 ..................... 54, 58, 60
search-help exit ............... 98
secure & controlled SAP environment ................. 66
Security - Material Master 61
Security Audit Log ........... 62
security objects ............... 113
Self-service password reset ..................................... 36
senior project person ....... 62
sensitive transaction ...... 107
SM04 .............................. 15
SM30 ............. 25, 27, 60, 104
SM35 ......................... 31, 80
SM35 guidelines ............. 80
SM59 ........................ 11, 31
Special Access .................. 81
special printing software .. 96
specific company code ..... 83
specific plant .................... 84
SPRO ...... 18, 23, 53, 104, 119
ST03 ............. 27, 39, 44, 63
standard end user reports ..................................... 103

Standard Menu ............. 100
standard text ..................... 61
Standard value * .............. 85
stock ................................ 91
structure ........ 67, 91, 92, 98
SU01 ... 12, 13, 16, 25, 28, 53, 56, 77, 81, 94, 97, 105, 115
SU01 transaction ............. 81
SU22 ............................... 50
SU25 ......................... 20, 21
SU50 ............................... 28
SUIM .. 12, 13, 14, 18, 20, 25, 37, 41, 50, 51, 63, 76
SUKRI ............................. 41
SUPER USER .................. 81
super-user access ............. 62
Super-user authority for emergencies ................. 62
Surveying departments ... 37
switch check/maintain .... 82
Sync function module ...... 77
system default ............... 100
system landscape ............ 64
system settings ............... 95
T500P .............................. 51
table dump ...................... 84
table maintenance ........... 99
Table names .................... 13
table UST12 .................... 76
TACT ......................... 13, 36
target ........... 37, 53, 88, 109
t-code ... 78, 79, 84, 103, 107, 112, 114
T-code specified display . 112
t-code SU24 .................... 79
T-codes O* ..................... 104
TCURR .......................... 53
TDD'S ............................ 86
technical info ................. 119
Time Data Administrator 74
time stamp ...................... 75
timestamp feature ........... 75

trace....18, 31, 32, 35, 46, 57, 78, 87, 110, 120
Tracing security authorizations ............. 78
track...................... 27, 62, 86
track and control ............ 62
Tracking user data ............27
Transaction code access .. 25
transaction data ................ 68
Transaction execution ..... 39
transaction inheritance feature........................... 87
transaction OOAC........... 110
Transaction Report - Roles ........................................76
transaction SCC4 .............. 71
transaction screen ..........106
transactions ..20, 25, 38, 39, 41, 45, 47, 52, 54, 58, 73, 75, 76, 86, 87, 91, 104, 112, 113, 114
Transfer authorizations... 88
transport Favorites ...........91
transport request ............109
trawl ...............................102
TSTC............................... 58
UCMON............................ 29
UMR ......................62, 88, 96
UMR's............................... 96

unauthorized transactions ........................................90
Underlying Generated Profile ............................97
unit testing........................86
up to date roles ..............109
Updating Organizational Levels in Profile Generator ................... 101
Upgrading issues .............. 21
Urgent - Authorization.....98
user authorizations .. 48, 56, 60, 78, 88
user buffer .........88, 114, 115
User comparison .............. 51
user defaults ....................28
user master compare..94, 97
User Menu Options ........100
user's authorizations ........78
valid to date .....................75
value is blank ...................69
variants ............................87
vendor master.................119
VF02 ................................36
Views> m_mat* .............. 61
WERKS .................... 84, 101
within a role..............76, 102
workbook .......................120
workplace shell................64

www.ingramcontent.com/pod-product-compliance
Lightning Source LLC
LaVergne TN
LVHW042338060326
832902LV00006B/248